LANGUAGE ARTS EXPLORER JUNIOR

How to Write a Business Letter

by Cecilia Minden
and Kate Roth

CHERRY LAKE PUBLISHING · ANN ARBOR, MICHIGAN

CHERRY LAKE

Publishing

Published in the United States of America by Cherry Lake Publishing
Ann Arbor, Michigan
www.cherrylakepublishing.com

Content Adviser: Gail Dickinson, PhD, Associate Professor, Old Dominion University, Norfolk, Virginia

Photo Credits: Page 6, ©Picsfive/Shutterstock, Inc.; page 8, ©NicoTucol/Shutterstock, Inc.; page 10, ©Susanne Neal/Dreamstime.com; page 14, ©Lisa F. Young/Dreamstime.com; page 17, ©Gelpi/Shutterstock, Inc.; page 19, ©Anke Van Wyk/Dreamstime.com

Library of Congress Cataloging-in-Publication Data
Minden, Cecilia.
  How to write a business letter / by Cecilia Minden and Kate Roth.
    p. cm. — (Language arts explorer junior)
  Includes bibliographical references and index.
  ISBN 978-1-61080-493-6 (lib. bdg.) — ISBN 978-1-61080-580-3 (e-book) — ISBN 978-1-61080-667-1 (pbk.)
1. Commercial correspondence—Juvenile literature. I. Roth, Kate. II. Title.
  HF5721.M56 2013
  651.7'5—dc23   2012008034

Cherry Lake Publishing would like to acknowledge the work of The Partnership for 21st Century Skills. Please visit www.21stcenturyskills.org for more information.

Printed in the United States of America
Corporate Graphics Inc.
July 2012
CLFA11

Table of Contents

CHAPTER ONE

Doing Business

Think of a product you like. A product is something that is made or sold. For example, maybe your favorite cereal is Great Oats. You want to tell the **business** that makes Great Oats how much you like their cereal. Everyone likes to hear they are doing a good job. You can write the company a business letter!

A business letter has six main parts:
1. **Heading** and date (letter writer's name and address and the date)
2. Inside address (name of the person you're writing to, his/her job title, name of the business, address)
3. **Greeting** (the words that begin the letter)
4. Body (the main part of the letter)

5. **Closing** (the words that end a letter)
6. **Signature** (the letter writer's first and last name, both printed and written by hand)

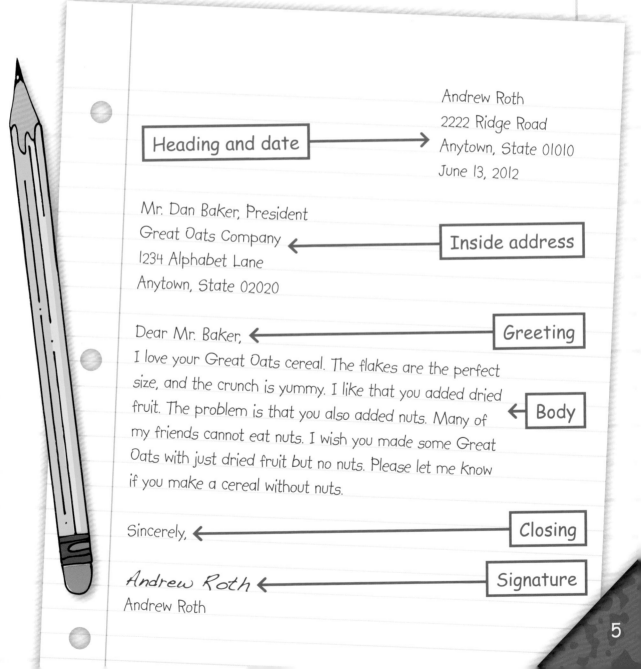

Heading and date → Andrew Roth
2222 Ridge Road
Anytown, State 01010
June 13, 2012

Mr. Dan Baker, President
Great Oats Company ← Inside address
1234 Alphabet Lane
Anytown, State 02020

Dear Mr. Baker, ← Greeting
I love your Great Oats cereal. The flakes are the perfect size, and the crunch is yummy. I like that you added dried fruit. The problem is that you also added nuts. Many of ← Body
my friends cannot eat nuts. I wish you made some Great Oats with just dried fruit but no nuts. Please let me know if you make a cereal without nuts.

Sincerely, ← Closing

Andrew Roth ← Signature
Andrew Roth

Writing a business letter is different from writing a letter to a friend. **Stationery** is paper used for letters. Business letters are written on plain white stationery. They are mailed in plain white **envelopes**.

Always make a **draft** of your letter. You can then copy it onto the stationery.

Plain white stationery makes your letter look professional.

You will only need a few supplies to write your letter.

Here is what you will need to complete the activities in this book:

- Blank notebook paper
- Plain white stationery and an envelope
- Stamp
- Pencil with an eraser
- Pen with blue or black ink
- A computer (optional)

CHAPTER TWO

What Do You Think?

You could write a letter to the makers of your favorite video game.

You can write to a business to let its employees know what you like or don't like. You can also write to ask questions. For example, Tom likes a certain computer game. He wants to know if there are other games like it. He needs to find out who makes the game and then write the company a business letter.

To get a copy of this activity, visit www.cherrylakepublishing.com/activities.

ACTIVITY

Choose Your Topic

In this activity you will choose the topic for your letter.

INSTRUCTIONS:
1. Make a list of products you might write about in a business letter.
2. Include products that you use often and strongly like or dislike.
3. Include products about which you have a question.
4. Choose one product for the topic of your letter.

- CarZ computer game—
  What other games are like it?

- Kenzie Backpack—
  Where can I buy it?

- Play Life toys—
  These toys have great themes, but the figures all look the same.

Ask a librarian to help you find the name of the business that makes the product you are writing about in your letter.

CHAPTER THREE

From Me to You

Companies are more likely to take your letter seriously if it is written in the proper format.

A business letter begins with a heading. The heading is the writer's name and address and today's date. It lets the business know where to send an answer to your letter. Write your name and address in the upper right-hand corner of your draft paper. Below the address, write the date you are sending the letter.

Heading and Date

In this activity you will write the heading and the date on your draft.

INSTRUCTIONS:
1. On a blank sheet of paper, write your heading in the upper right-hand corner.
2. Write your name on the first line.
3. Write your street address on the second line.
4. Write your city, state, and zip code on the third line.
5. Write today's date below your address on the fourth line.

To get a copy of this activity, visit www.cherrylakepublishing.com/activities.

Spell out the name of the month. For example, write February 10, 2012, not 2/10/12.

Annabel Roth
88 Wood Lane
Anytown, State 01010
September 25, 2012

CHAPTER FOUR

Dear Sir or Madam

Next, write the inside address. This is the name and address of the business. Are you writing to a specific person? Be sure to include that person's title. For example: *Mr. Dan Baker, President.*

Write the greeting below the address. For example: *Dear Mr. Baker.* If you do not know who will read the letter, then write *Dear Sir or Madam.*

Do you know the name of the person you're writing to?

Dear Si

Inside Address and Greeting

In this activity you will write the inside address and the greeting on your draft.

INSTRUCTIONS:

1. Leave some space between the heading and the inside address.
2. Write the inside address. This is the name and address of the business.
3. Write the person's name and title on the first line.
4. Write his or her address below the name.
5. Write the greeting Dear Sir or Madam or the person's name.

To get a copy of this activity, visit www.cherrylakepublishing.com/activities.

Annabel Roth
88 Wood Lane
Anytown, State 01010
September 25, 2012

Best Toy Company
2 Toy Avenue
Anytown, State 01010

Dear Sir or Madam,

To Whom It May Concern can also be used as a greeting when you aren't sure who will read your letter.

CHAPTER FIVE

I Wanted You to Know

If you are writing to a video game company, you might want to take notes on your favorite parts of the game.

What would you like the company to know? Try to think of three things. First, let them know what you think about their product. Next, let them know why you are writing. Finally, let them know what you want them to do.

For example, Tom might begin by writing about how much he likes the video game CarZ. He could tell the company that he likes to play the game with his friends. Next, he would write his question, asking if there are other games like CarZ. Finally, Tom would ask the business to write and let him know where he could buy the other games.

ACTIVITY

Body of the Letter

In this activity, you will write the message of your letter.

INSTRUCTIONS:
1. Begin by writing what you think of the product.
2. Next, explain why you are writing. Do you have a question to ask? Are you writing to report that the product is great or not so great?
3. Finally, write what you want the business to do.

Activity continued on page 16.

Activity continued from page 15.

Annabel Roth
88 Wood Lane
Anytown, State 01010
September 25, 2012

Best Toy Company
2 Toy Avenue
Anytown, State 01010

Dear Sir or Madam,
All the kids in my family love to play with Play Life toys. Each set has a great theme, such as farm and pirates. I like that there are so many small parts for each theme. Your toy is fun for boys and girls.

I think there is one problem with your toy. All of the play figures in your sets have brown eyes and a brown mouth. I wish you made people with different color eyes. I think more mouths should be red. I hope you will consider adding different play figures when you create new sets.

CHAPTER SIX

Sincerely

Your signature adds a personal touch to the letter.

The end of the letter is called the closing. Most business letters end with *Sincerely* or *Yours truly*. Leave a space below the closing and print your full name. Then sign your name above your printed name. Why write it two times? One is your signature, so the business knows you wrote the letter. The printed name below makes sure your name is clearly written.

for boys and girls.

I think there is one problem with your toy. All of the play figures in your sets have brown eyes and a brown mouth. I wish you made people with different color eyes. I think more mouths should be red. I hope you will consider adding different play figures when you create new sets.

Appreciatively,

Andrew Roth

Andrew Roth

Always use an ink pen to sign your business letters.

ACTIVITY

Closing and Signature

In this activity you will finish the draft of your letter.

INSTRUCTIONS:
1. Choose a closing for your letter. Here are some sample closings for a business letter:
   - Sincerely
   - Yours truly
   - Appreciatively
2. Put a comma at the end of the closing.
3. Sign your first and last name below the closing.
4. Print your first and last name below the signature.

To get a copy of this activity, visit www.cherrylakepublishing.com/activities.

CHAPTER SEVEN

In the Mail

Hopefully you will get a letter back from the business where you sent your letter.

After you finish your draft, check your spelling. When the letter is just right, copy it to the white stationery. Be sure to use your best handwriting! Address an envelope by writing your address in the upper left-hand corner of the envelope. Write the business address in the middle of the envelope. Don't forget to add a stamp!

To get a copy of this activity, visit www.cherrylakepublishing.com/activities.

ACTIVITY

Writing the Final Copy and Addressing an Envelope

In this activity you will write the final copy and address the envelope.

INSTRUCTIONS:

1. Copy your letter onto the white stationery in your neatest handwriting. You can also use a computer to type your final letter.
2. If you use a computer, print out your letter and sign your name by hand.
3. Address the envelope. Be sure to write on the front of the envelope. The **seal flap** should be at the top of the back side.
4. Write your name and address in the upper left-hand corner of the envelope.
5. Write the name and address of the business in the center of the envelope.
6. Put a stamp in the upper right-hand corner of the envelope.

Annabel Roth
88 Wood Lane
Anytown, State 01010

Best Toy Company
2 Toy Avenue
Anytown, State 01010

To get a copy of this activity, visit www.cherrylakepublishing.com/activities.

ACTIVITY

Final Changes

Read the instructions carefully. Check everything one more time.

☐ YES ☐ NO Do I start my letter with a heading and today's date?

☐ YES ☐ NO Do I include an inside address?

☐ YES ☐ NO Do I include a greeting?

☐ YES ☐ NO Do I include a closing and signature?

☐ YES ☐ NO Do I address the envelope correctly?

☐ YES ☐ NO Do I remember to put a stamp on the envelope?

Now you can wait for the business to write you back. While you are waiting, you can try writing to more companies. What other businesses will receive your letters?

Glossary

body (BAH-dee) the main part of a letter

business (BIZ-niss) an organization that makes, buys, or sells something to make money

closing (KLOH-zing) the words that end a letter

draft (DRAFT) a first version of a document, or one that is not final

envelopes (ON-vuh-lohpss) flat paper coverings that are used to mail letters

greeting (GREE-ting) the opening words of a letter, such as "Dear Sir"

heading (HED-ing) the writer's name, address, and date written at the top of a business letter

product (PRAH-dukt) something that is created, made, or produced

seal flap (SEEL FLAP) the part of an envelope that folds down to close it

signature (SIG-nuh-chur) a person's name signed by hand

stationery (STAY-shuh-ner-ee) special paper used for letter writing

For More Information

BOOK
Loewen, Nancy. *Sincerely Yours: Writing Your Own Letter.*
Minneapolis: Picture Window Books, 2009.

WEB SITE
International Reading Association—Read Write Think
www.readwritethink.org/classroom-resources/student-interactives/
letter-generator-30005.html
Generate your own letters with this handy guide.

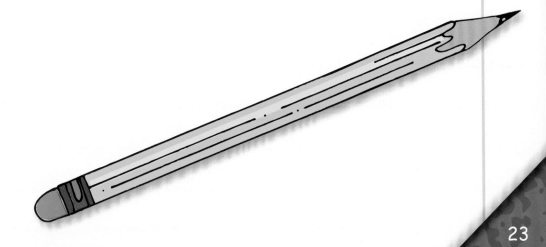

Index

About the Authors

Cecilia Minden, PhD, is the former director of the Language and Literacy Program at Harvard Graduate School of Education. She earned her doctorate from the University of Virginia. While at Harvard, Dr. Minden also taught several writing courses. Her research focused on early literacy skills and developing phonics curricula. She is now an educational consultant and the author of more than 100 books for children. Dr. Minden lives with her family in Chapel Hill, North Carolina. She likes to write early in the morning while the house is still quiet.

Kate Roth has a doctorate from Harvard University in language and literacy and a master's from Columbia University Teachers College in curriculum and teaching. Her work focuses on writing instruction in the primary grades. She has taught first grade, kindergarten, and Reading Recovery. She has also instructed hundreds of teachers from around the world in early literacy practices. She lives in Shanghai, China, with her husband and three children, ages 3, 7, and 10. Her oldest two children, Annabel and Andrew, wrote the letters used in this book.